# The Great GRAPH Contest

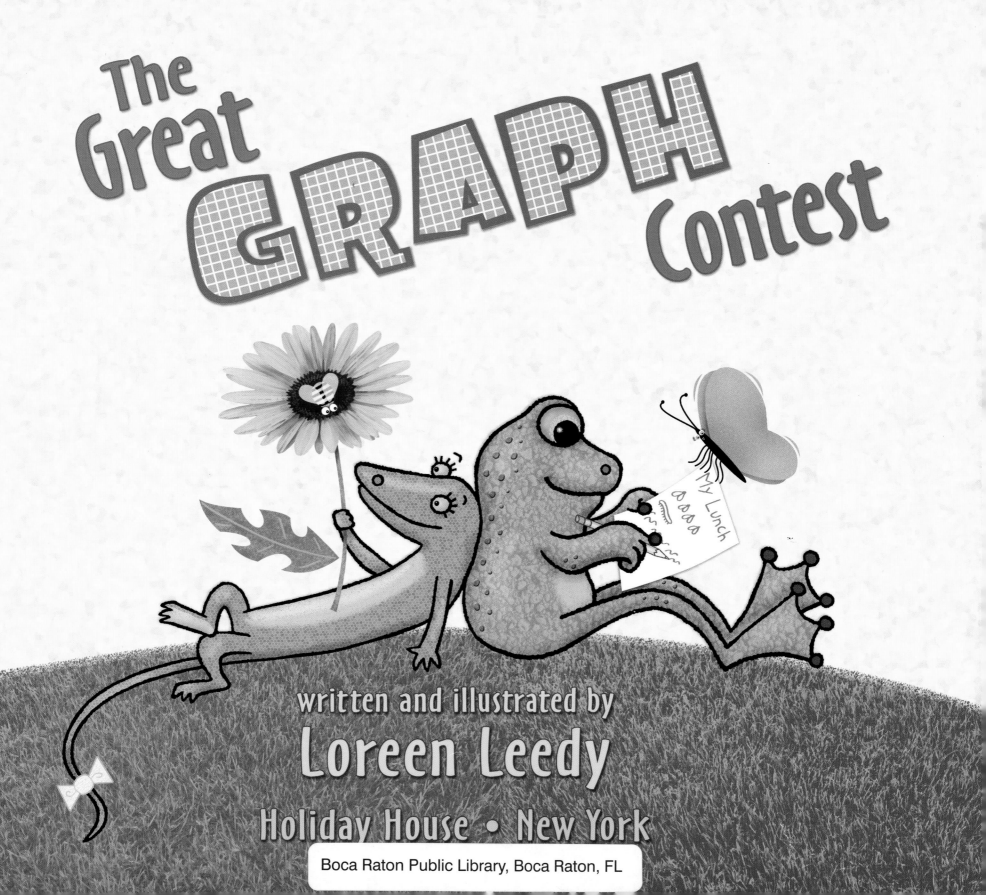

written and illustrated by
## Loreen Leedy

### Holiday House • New York

Thanks to Martha H. Hopkins, Ph.D. and NBCT, of
the College of Education at the University of Central
Florida, for commenting on the text and sketches.

Manufactured in China    www.holidayhouse.com

3 5 7 9 10 8 6 4 2

Library of Congress Cataloging-in-Publication Data
Leedy, Loreen. The great graph contest /
written and illustrated by Loreen Leedy. – 1st ed.  p. cm.
Summary: Gonk and Chester, two amphibian friends,
hold a contest to see who can make better graphs.
ISBN 0-8234-1710-7
[1. Graphic methods – Fiction. 2. Amphibians – Fiction.] I. Title.
PZ7.L51524Gp 2004          [E] – dc22          2003062549
ISBN-13: 978-0-8234-1710-0 (hardcover)    ISBN-10: 0-8234-1710-7 (hardcover)
ISBN-13: 978-0-8234-2029-2 (paperback)    ISBN-10: 0-8234-2029-9 (paperback)

Flowers

Here is a Venn diagram. The suits with **flowers** are in the left circle.

# More About GRAPHS

Let's take a look at some of the graphs Gonk and Beezy made for the contest:

Pages 8-9: Gonk saw that some of the rocks were smooth and the rest were rough. To find out if there were more smooth or rough rocks, he grouped the smooth ones on one square and the rough on the other square. He made labels for the graph's title and for the two groups of rocks. It is easy to see that more of the rocks are smooth. But if a similar number of rocks were on each square, it would be hard to tell which group was larger; you would have to count all of the rocks. This quantity graph has two squares, but some have three, four, or more sections.

Are more rocks smooth or rough?

Smooth | Rough

Pages 10-13: This bar graph is also made of real objects, cookies in this case. To see which kind of cookie was most common, Beezy piled up each type in a separate stack. If a stack is taller, that means there are more of those cookies. (The cookies must be about the same thickness for the results to be accurate.) The graph shows there are more chocolate chip cookies than the other two kinds.

Are there more chocolate chip, oatmeal, or sugar cookies?

Sugar | Oatmeal | Chocolate Chip

Pages 15-17: Venn diagrams show how things are alike and different. Gonk wanted to find out which pattern was the most popular on the bathing suits. He formed two big circles of string, making them overlap in the middle. He put the flowered suits in the left circle, the ones with a bug pattern in the right circle, and suits with both flowers and bugs in the overlap. As with all graphs, it is important to put labels on it so people understand what the graph is about.

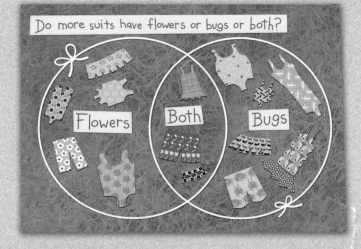

Do more suits have flowers or bugs or both?

Flowers | Both | Bugs

Pages 19-20: For this circle graph, Beezy cut a paper circle into twelve equal wedges (for each of the twelve butterflies). She drew a butterfly on each piece. Then she colored one wedge purple for the purple butterfly, two blue for the blue butterflies, and so on. She arranged the pieces back into a circle, putting the same colors next to one another. The graph shows that orange is the most common color in this group of butterflies.

What color is most common?

Duck         |
Snake        |||
Songbird     ||
Turtle       ||||
Hummingbird  |||

Pages 22-23: Gonk collected data about the kind of animal that was hatching out and how many of each. He cut out paper rectangles (all the same size) and drew a picture of each baby. He put the babies in one of two groups, either reptiles or birds. He lined up the pictures in two rows on poster board cut into an egg shape. The graph shows that more reptiles hatched than birds. This is a horizontal version of a bar graph.

Did more reptiles or birds hatch?
Reptiles
Birds

Pages 24-27: Beezy took a survey to find out what shoppers planned to do with their new flowers. She wrote down their answers to keep track of the data. She made a tulip shape out of poster board and then wrote the title question on top. The vertical line has equally spaced numbers and the label "Number of shoppers." The horizontal line has the three answers the shoppers gave. To complete this bar graph, she made flower shapes (all the same size but in three colors) and for each answer put a color-coded flower in its correct column.

Survey Question:
what will you do with
your new flower?
chipmunk: plant it
slug: give it away
bunny: plant it
caterpillar: eat it
guinea pig: plant it
mole: give it away
woodchuck: plant it
squirrel: give it away
tortoise: eat it

What do shoppers plan to do with their new flower?
Number of shoppers
0 1 2 3 4 5
Plant it   Give it away   Eat it

# Make Your Own GRAPHS

Graphs are a great way to organize information, find out something, and display it visually. The graphs in this book are based on these types:

## QUANTITY GRAPH

It may have two, three, or more equally sized sections.

## CIRCLE GRAPH

The sections may be equal, but they don't have to be. Also known as a pie chart.

## VENN DIAGRAM

It has two or more overlapping circles (or other shapes).

## BAR GRAPH

The bars (which can be rows of pictures or symbols) can go horizontally or vertically.

**1** To make your own graph, think of a question to ask.

What is my family's favorite snack food?

**2** Collect data and write it down.

Snack Data
Mom: dried worms
Dad: fried flies
Tunk: cricket legs
Me: fried flies
Gran: cricket legs
Bink: fried flies

**3** Use real objects and/or art supplies to create your graph.

My Family's Favorite Snack Food
🪰 fried flies
〰 cricket legs
🪱 dried worms

**4** Put a title and labels on your graph so people will know what it is about.

Your family likes fried flies the best!